Making Line Graphs

By Mary Molly Shea

Gareth Stevens
PUBLISHING

leveled reader
math

Please visit our website, www.garethstevens.com. For a free color catalog of all our high-quality books, call toll free 1-800-542-2595 or fax 1-877-542-2596.

Library of Congress Cataloging-in-Publication Data

Shea, Mary Molly.
Making line graphs / by Mary Molly Shea.
  p. cm. — (Graph it!)
Includes index.
ISBN 978-1-4824-0835-5 (pbk.)
ISBN 978-1-4824-0836-2 (6-pack)
ISBN 978-1-4824-0834-8 (library binding)
1. Graphic methods — Juvenile literature. 2. Mathematics — Charts, diagrams, etc. — Juvenile literature. 3. Mathematical statistics — Graphic methods — Juvenile literature. I. Shea, Mary Molly. II.Title.
QA40.5 S44 2015
510—d23

Published in 2015 by
Gareth Stevens Publishing
111 East 14th Street, Suite 349
New York, NY 10003

Copyright © 2015 Gareth Stevens Publishing

Designer: Katelyn E. Reynolds
Editor: Therese Shea

Photo credits: Cover, pp. 1–24 (background texture) ctrlaplus/Shutterstock.com; cover, pp. 1, 5, 7, 9, 11, 13, 17, 19, 21 (line graph elements) Colorlife/Shutterstock.com; p. 17 (photo) racom/Shutterstock.com.

Printed in the United States of America

CPSIA compliance information: Batch #CS15GS: For further information contact Gareth Stevens, New York, New York at 1-800-542-2595.

Contents

Boldface words appear in the glossary.

Learning from Lines

Graphs help us **compare** facts. Many line graphs show changes in facts over time. For example, you could show your height each year on a line graph. Let's learn more about line graphs and make our own!

My Height

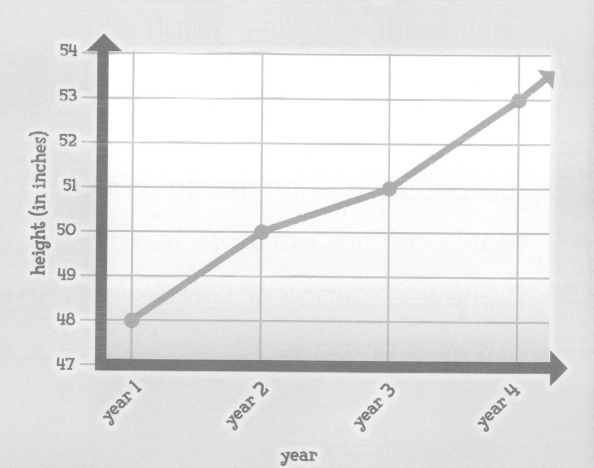

Each point on a line graph is a fact. On this line graph, a point shows the number of puppies in the pet store each month. Which month did the pet store have the fewest puppies? Check your answers on page 22.

6

Pet Store Puppies

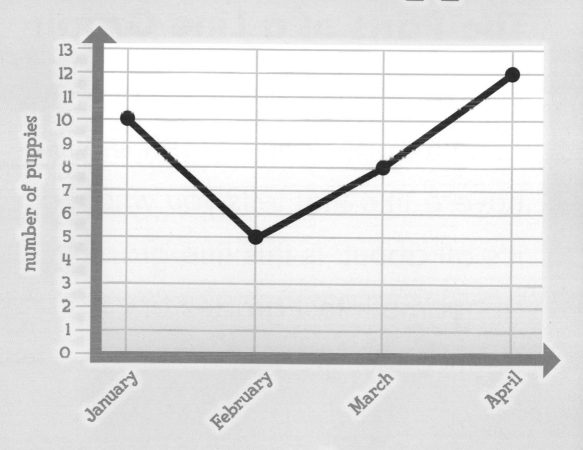

The Parts of a Line Graph

Line graphs are made up of certain parts. A line graph should have a title that tells you what it's all about. Is this line graph about math test grades or science test grades?

Math Test Grades

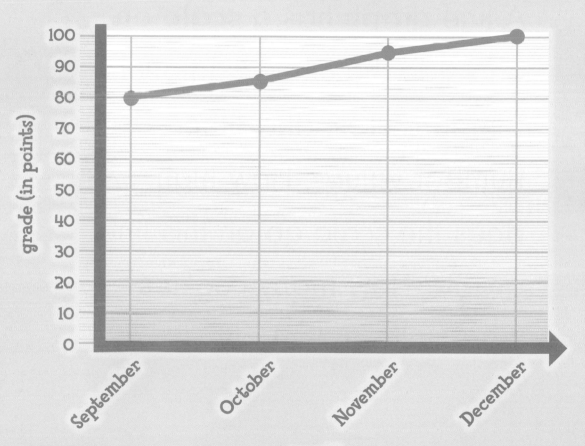

A line graph has a **scale** on one side that shows amounts, temperatures, and other number values. How high does the scale go on this line graph? How many cookies were sold on Sunday?

10

Cookies Sold

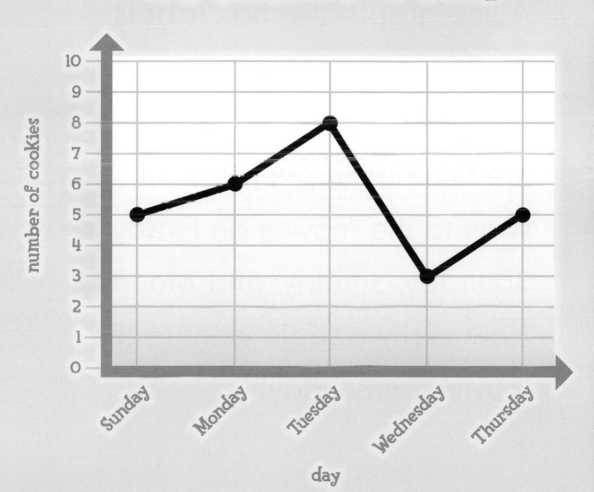

A line graph also has **labels** that tell what kinds of facts are given. This graph is about the number of people who went to the movies on Friday, Saturday, Sunday, and Monday. How many people went to the movies on Sunday?

How Many Went to the Movies?

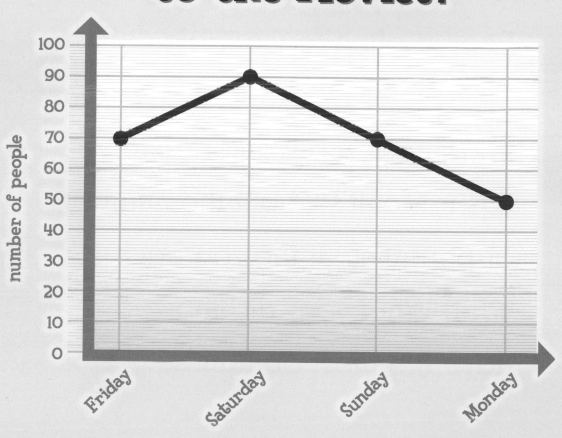

Graphing with Penguins

People often make tables of facts before they make a graph. Imagine a zoo worker gave you this table. It's about the number of penguins at the zoo each year. What year did the zoo have the most penguins?

Penguins at the Zoo

year	number of penguins
2006	5
2008	8
2010	9
2012	6
2014	10

Make a line graph using the table on page 15. Draw it on a piece of paper. One side of the graph should be labeled "year" and include each year in the table. The other side should say "number of penguins." Don't forget a scale with numbers!

number of penguins

12
11
10
9
8
7
6
5
4
3
2
1
0

2006   2008   2010   2012   2014

year

Mark points on the graph. The points are the number of penguins living at the zoo each year. Connect the points. Last, give the graph a title. Does your graph look like this? How many more penguins were in the zoo in 2014 than 2012?

Penguins at the Zoo

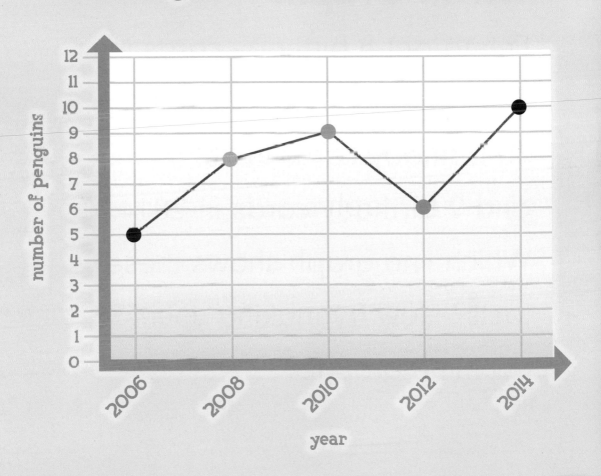

Which Graph?

Emma got 5 birthday cards in 2011, 8 birthday cards in 2012, 10 birthday cards in 2013, and 9 birthday cards in 2014. Which line graph shows these facts? Now try making your own line graph!

Birthday Cards

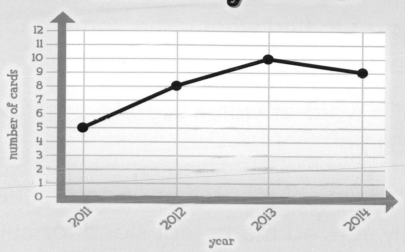

Birthday Cards

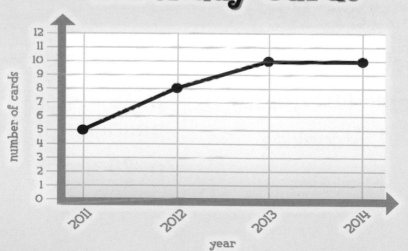

Glossary

compare: to find what is the same and what is different about two or more things

label: a word or words used to describe something

scale: a way of measuring using a series of equally spaced marks that stand for numbers

Answer Key

p. 6 February

p. 8 math test grades

p. 10 10, 5 cookies

p. 12 70 people

p. 14 2014

p. 18 4 more penguins

p. 20 graph on top

For More Information

Books

Besel, Jennifer M. *Lions and Tigers and Graphs! Oh My!* Mankato, MN: Capstone Press, 2011.

Cocca, Lisa Colozza. *Line Graphs.* Ann Arbor, MI: Cherry Lake Publishing, 2013.

Edgar, Sherra G. *Line Graphs.* Ann Arbor, MI: Cherry Lake Publishing, 2013.

Websites

Create Line Graphs
www.ixl.com/math/grade-3/create-line-graphs
Practice making a line graph using a table of facts.

Line Graphs
www.mathsisfun.com/data/line-graphs.html
See how a table or chart can be made into a line graph.

Make Your Own Line Graph
mrnussbaum.com/graph/line/
Use this site to make your own line graph.

Index

24